Rising Venus

Rising Venus

poems

Kelly Cherry

LOUISIANA STATE UNIVERSITY PRESS

BATON ROUGE   2002

Manufactured in the United States of America
First printing
11   10   09   08   07   06   05   04   03   02
5   4   3   2   1

Designer: Laura Roubique Gleason
Typeface: Minion text with Shelley Volante display
Printer and binder: Thomson-Shore, Inc.

Library of Congress Cataloging-in-Publication Data:

Cherry, Kelly.
  Rising Venus: poems / Kelly Cherry.
    p.   cm.
  ISBN 0-8071-2767-1 (alk. paper) — ISBN 0-8071-2768-x (pbk. : alk. paper)
  1. Women—Poetry. I. Title.
  PS3553.H357 R57 2002
  811'.54—dc21

2001005168

The paper in this book meets the guidelines for permanence and durability
of the Committee on Production Guidelines for Book Longevity of the
Council on Library Resources. ∞

Acknowledgments

Grateful acknowledgment is made to the editors of the following publications, in which some of the poems in this book first appeared (sometimes in earlier versions or under other titles):

Atlanta Review: "Sunrise" (as "Day on the River"); *Calapooya Collage:* "Catching Hell"; *Christianity and Literature:* "Virgin and Child"; *Cortland Review* (an Internet journal): "She Doesn't Care What You Say about Her So Long as You Spell Her Name Right"; *Crosscurrents:* "Facing the Truth about Yourself," "My House"; *Cumberland Poetry Review:* "Lunch at the Lake"; *Dark Horse Literary Review:* "Art and Life"; *Denver Quarterly:* "In the Place Where the Corridors Watch Your Every Move"; *Four Quarters:* "Lament of the Gorgon," "Nobody's Fool"; *Gettysburg Review:* "On Looking at a Yellow Wagon"; *Graven Images:* "The Cypress (Fiesole)," "A Frame of Mind," "Wishing I Could Bring You Back and See Things More Clearly This Time Around"; *Image:* "On Looking at a Painting by van Gogh"; *Kenyon Review:* "The Model Looks at Her Portrait: A Retrospective," "Rising Venus"; *Laurel Review:* "Crackers"; *New Letters:* "American Movies," "The Color Red," "Romantic Art"; *Pivot:* "An Other Woman" (as "Other Woman"); *Poetry:* "Study for an Annunciation"; *Rubicon:* "Lady Macbeth on the Psych Ward"; *Sequoia:* "Bat Mother"; *Shenandoah:* "Battle Scene," "The Horse at Dusk"; *Windhover:* "The Grecian Grace of a White Egret" (as "For a Child of the Bayou"); *Transactions:* "The Final Visit with Her Brother"; *Women's Review of Books:* "Adult Ed. 101: Basic Home Repair for Single Women," "Becoming My Mother."

"My House" was reprinted in *Anthology of Magazine Verse and Yearbook of American Poetry,* ed. A. F. Pater (Monitor, 1985). "In the Place Where the Corridors Watch Your Every Move" was reprinted in *Articulations: The Body and Illness in Poetry,* ed. Jon Mukand (University of Iowa Press, 1994). "Rothko" first appeared in *Wisconsin Poets at the Elvehjem Museum of Art,* ed. Patricia Powell (University of Wisconsin, 1995). "Lunch at the Lake" was reprinted in *Bite to Eat Place,* ed. Andrea Adolph, Donald L. Vallis, and Anne F. Walker (Redwood Coast, 1995). "Lady Macbeth on the Psych Ward" was reprinted in *The*

Muse Strikes Back, ed. Katherine McAlpine and Gail White (Story Line, 1997). "Lady Macbeth on the Psych Ward" and "Adult Ed. 101: Basic Home Repair for Single Women" were reprinted in *A New Pléiade* by Seven American Poets (Louisiana State University Press, 1998). "The Model Looks at Her Portrait: A Retrospective" was reprinted in *Betty Watson Paintings: Five Decades* (Odalisque, 1999). "Becoming My Mother" was reprinted in *Mothers and Daughters,* ed. June Cotner (Harmony, 2001).

"Adult Ed. 101: Basic Home Repair for Single Women," "My House," "Sappho in Her Study" (as "The Room in Which I Write"), "Nobody's Fool," "Facing the Truth about Yourself," "S.A.D.," "Catching Hell," "Bat Mother," "Becoming My Mother," "Crackers," "Lament of the Gorgon," "In the Place Where the Corridors Watch Your Every Move," "Lady Macbeth on the Psych Ward," and "The Final Visit with Her Brother" were included in the chapbook *Time Out of Mind* (March Street, 1994). "An Other Woman" was published as a chapbook (limited edition) with that title (Somers Rocks, 2000).

The author thanks Barbara Silver and the Weatherspoon Art Gallery for permission to reproduce the image of *Small Venus* (formerly identified as *Rising Venus*), a sculpture by Jonathan Silver.

Contents

I

The Bat that flits at close of Eve
Has left the Brain that won't Believe.

—William Blake, "Auguries of Innocence"

. . . something is amiss or out of place
When mice with wings can wear a human face.

—Theodore Roethke, "The Bat"

The bat got so excited his fur stood up straight and he felt warm all
over. He thought: "I'll go to the chipmunk and say, 'If you'll give
me six crickets I'll make a poem about you.' Really I'd do it for
nothing; but they don't respect something if they get it for nothing.
I'll say: 'For six crickets I'll do your portrait in verse.'"

—Randall Jarrell, *The Bat-Poet*

Adult Ed. 101: Basic Home Repair for Single Women

The Tool Box

should contain utility knife
trouble light
curved-claw hammer
wrench
and rib-joint pliers.

A little putty helps.

Hacksaw and coping saw (coping saw!)
caulking gun
screwdrivers (with orange juice)—

Don't forget those rib-joint pliers.

The Power Drill

is a prerequisite for almost anything
you may wish to do: hang curtains,
pictures of your last lover,
your last lover.

Some Nails

Common ones have a large head, thick shaft. Good for the widest
variety of purposes. Box nails are thinner and may be used where
the common nail would cause splits. Roofing nails have an extra
large head and barbed shaft. The spiral shank of the screw-nail gives
it a tenacious grip. Duplex nails are temporary. Do not expect a du-
plex nail to hold permanently. This is a mistake many women make.

Types of Screws

The two universal slot designs are the straight slot and the Phillips.
Both are available in most types of screws. Look for bright steel,
dipped, galvanized, brass- or chrome-plated and solid brass screws.
Stainless steel screws are also made but they are not always easy to
find.

From time to time, you may have to call in a professional.

Painting the Ceiling

Wear goggles and mask when painting the ceiling
or going anywhere your ex-lover may be seen with his new wife.

A roller with a splash shield is also good,
whether you paint with latex
or heart's blood.

Drywall

Studs should be sixteen inches apart
but are often fewer and farther between
and let's face it, you may have seen your last stud.
In that case, use an anchor
in plaster or drywall
and repair minor cracks
by filling the voids.
Feather each coat of spackle into the surrounding area
to help hide the seam.
Soon the surface will be flawless.

Plumbing

The shit goes down the drain.

Class Commencement

Now you can begin
to put your house in order:
caulk your windows against incoming drafts,
drain outside faucets, dig up bulbs.
Prepare your bed.
Clouds are blowing in from the west, over the lake.
Winter is on its way.

Ladies, you are about to find out
just how much really rough
weather
your house can take.

About the Men

A woman learns to be hard
up North. There's just so much work to it all:
icicles black as night in a cave
on the far side of the moon
clinging to the underside of the car,
a bullying wind off the lake
making you hunch your shoulders,
keep your head down.

And that's only the weather.

What about the men
who have never held a woman close
in a garden
behind a house
where passionflowers covered the mortared brick
like kissy smacks of bright red lipstick?

Man on the Hall

There wasn't a single girl who'd not fly off
like a scared wren, but left her dorm room door
open a crack to hear and see what rough
beast was slouching toward the emptied floor,
and when the guy was gone and the all-clear sounded,
we all flew back to ask one another
if he was taken—or was he someone's brother
(which meant *available*)? If dumped, rebounded?
Pre-med? Or law? It was a kind of cooing
we made, we girls with our talk of wooing.

How to imagine now the maddening feeling
of being worth less than a man? The ceiling
's in shards.
          —It was not easy. Our lives bled
on the books we wrote, some you may have read.

My House

First, the hall.

On a wall in a room to the right,
a moon by Magritte hangs from a tree like a leaf.

Birds fly over the pillows.
Sunlight falls downstairs.

The study is small and scumbled with revisions.
My bedroom is not quite masterful.

All night, and the books on their shelves are leaning
toward one another in search of meaning.

Sappho in Her Study

The files in the filing cabinet
Are all talking at once.
Mumble jumble, say the files
In the filing cabinet.

The desk, discreet,
Discloses nothing.

Rough drafts live
A roustabout life,
Tumbling from shelves,

While books, published
And smugly replete,
No longer feel the need
To compete.

Stationery sprawls,
Casual as sunbathers.

In the locked drawer,
Love letters lie.

Lunch at the Lake

Bees are falling out of the sky,
Thick and heavy as honey.
The lake is as sour as rye.

Curdling in late summer, the lake
Is as sluggish as cream. Fish bake.
The sun is the color of a cornflake.

Fish float in on waves, already broiled.
They lie on their sides, dead to the world.
Your own skin's well oiled.

You could die and be eaten, here
On the lakeshore wall, where
Bees are streaming through your hair

And fish are serving themselves up
On your lap, poisoned, and the paper cup
You sip from is alive, says the environmental commission, with
    denizens of the deep.

You could bob in the lake like ice cream in Coke,
Browned cow, melt in the sun, and sink.
You could drown yourself in the drink.

Stoic

The energy goes out.
Now there's nothing left—
it's a complete rout,
and you are bereft

of love, work, hope.
You do what you have to
(you know how to cope)
but there's nothing you cleave to

anymore, not even the old dream
of whatever it was
that used to seem
(it no longer does)

at least as urgent as a need to pee.
You're dry
as a dead sea,
might as well die.

Virginia Woolf's Last Suicide Note

Cannot go on—
Am drowning,
Fast as a stone.
People in high places are frowning,

Say *Yes you can*
And *Others do.*
But the indefatigable river
Is having its say too,

Says *These shaped and finny lights you thought*
Were fish
Are lives of women I caught.
My net was their wish

For love, truth, beauty and kindness.
Now they drift, mindless
As seaweed
Or Onan's spilled seed,

Forever,
Plying the waters
Between now and never,
Neptune's drydocked daughters.

Nobody's Fool

Gazing down
that dark well.
A good-looking man pushed me—
in I fell.

Walls of gloom,
stink of damp.
Wish I'd brought
my Coleman lamp.

Down I go,
no moss on my back.
Will it never end?
Will I ever get back?

Wait, here's water,
black as a bruise.
I may take
a long cruise,

I just might choose
to live here forever.
You think I've got
a head full of fever

but let me say this—
nobody fools
a woman who's plumbed
her own depths. (And hell's.)

Facing the Truth about Yourself

It's coded, like a genetic deficiency.
It savages the heart like a disease,
Brings you to your knees.

Facing it, your face sags like a punctured balloon.
You are simultaneously tensed and paralyzed.
You can't claim you're surprised,

Quite, since you knew it all along.
But how will you stand the fear, the fear
And the emptiness? Let me make myself perfectly clear

About this last point. Nothing in the world
Will help, because the world is not real
Enough to contain even all that you do not feel

And what you feel is an absence
Of being, so spreading and here, it is as if everyone thought you
     died
Of a sickness, but you are as painfully alive as a bride

Unmet at the altar.
You are dressed in shame, you wear
Your great failure like seed pearls in your hair.

S.A.D.

Days when the world seems begrimed,
You too. Snow like stale white bread.
Days when the world is a stalled car, a battery gone dead.

And all that was yours—lost.
All that you loved—gone. Your heart, a crust.
Days you somehow weather in bed,

Unmoving, beyond even shame, even despair.
Waking or sleeping—it's all the same.
And hunger—nothing new there,

Either, it's all the same, the same.
You know this hunger so well, it is like knowing it by name.
And nothing can help. And you don't care.

She Doesn't Care What You Say about Her
So Long as You Spell Her Name Right

Would she have fame?
Would she take tea and have fame with her tea?
Or roll a joint, famously?

She imagined approval, applause,
A man not bored by her voracity.

In the house to be
Furnished in the future,
There would be intricate, quiet rugs,
Acres of books,
Someone playing the cello.

A late supper after the concert or play. . . .
Outside, the people were clamoring for autographs.

The Madonna Syndrome:

Later, they went home,
And the man who was not bored
By the fact that she loved him
Allowed her to write her name
On his balls with the tip
Of her tongue as many times
As it took to make sure
He got it right.

Catching Hell

Can anyone help me find
Time that is out of my mind?
I can't even remember
Who fucked me, or whose member
I sucked, whose book I signed

Scrawling my name across the page
As if I were not being eaten up by rage,
My brain being bit
By the ambition-gnat,
Feverish with that old contagion.

Whose penis did I squat on,
Or want to? This is not one
Of your rhetorical questions.
God knows how many sessions
With the doctor, his unclean breath hot on

My neck, haven't brought back
The time I lost when the bottom of the grocery sack
That is my mind fell out.
I should have caught
It; I caught hell. A huge Mack

Truck nearly ran over me
When I came to: I was crossing University
Against the light.
Next, it was night,
And someone who was not me

Rose out of my sleep,
Jangling her bracelets, and began to leap
About the room.
I watched her carom
Off the wall like a cue ball, I could barely keep

Her in my line of sight.
This devil danced all night.
When I woke, time was dead;
It had been killed. That devil had fled.
Time's body bled in the cold bright light.

Bat Mother

A bat flew out of my ear,
Saying, *Disappear! Disappear!*
I shut my eyes so no one could see me.
My lashes grew as long as wings.
I became my other self:

Dancing girl, child of surprising good cheer,
Full of rage, full of fear,
But hear how she sings
For her supper—eye of newt, wool-wing of bat.
Slip it in her bubbling vat

And never say she never did you a turn,
Mister Anybody. As for me,
I've got a little money to burn
And time on my hands and murder on my mind.
Just let me recollect who it was I killed.

(She was a young woman with a child.)

Becoming My Mother

And suddenly it's her voice I'm speaking
with, it's her look that's in my eye, and I
can feel it there, as if her face were my
face, and even the gestures I am making
are ones that were characteristic of her—
an absent twisting of a strand of hair,
a hand across her mouth, a decided air
of disapproval or despair, whichever
she felt, because she was never any good
at hiding what she felt—and there we're different,
since one thing I learned was to be diffident,
my role, forever, not mother- but child- hood.
    But now I find myself becoming her;
    childless though I am, my own mother.

Art and Life

In the hot house, the babies
Planted on their pots
Grow as quick as amaryllis,

Spiky and upspringing.
Their mother is the mother of imagery.
Soon

The babies will bloom.
Soon the white stars
Wavering in the night-wind

Like christening gowns
Laundered and dazzling
Will be taken down and folded

Flat and put away.
Day,
Prosy day,

That perfectionist critic
That reviews a woman and writes
Her off,

Discloses the empty house, the manless bed,
A carpet littered with the blood-red petals
Of the unborn dead.

Crackers

My mind is breaking,
Coming apart
Like my heart.
It is breaking

In two,
Crumbling into bits—
O my Ritz
Cracker of a brain! Bats flew

Out of my belfry.
I saw them hanging from the walls,
Hundreds of brown bats.
I could almost decipher their sonic calls,
Tickle their bite-sized bat-balls.

They were talking about me;
Now the subject's been changed.
I'm much too deranged
To be of interest, you see,

And the tower they left
Is split and down.
I've an ache in my head, a thorn in my crown.
Bereft,
Bereft,

Night flashes its wings—
Leathery and verminous,
Long black ungrammatical dashes—

Swoops into my brain.
It attaches itself upside down
To a crack in my skull; sense has flown.
(I can't even be sure I'm not sane.)

Lament of the Gorgon

I am the person
Who does not know
That other person
Who can come and go

In and out of my head.
I am the person
Who is out of her head.
Who is that person

Who lives in my head
When I am out of my head?
She won't let me in.
I bang on the door of my head,

I hit my head with my fists
Again and again,
Begging to be
Let in.

Go away, I shout
To the person
In my head,
But she won't

Let me in.
I don't even know her name.
The one time I saw her, her hair
Was ribboned with snakes.

Her braids hissed.
Two snakes kissed
A deadly kiss.
I'd have fled, but where?

Those snakes slithered through her hair.
Where where where
Can I go
When I am out of my head?

In the Place Where the Corridors Watch Your Every Move

In the place where the corridors watch your every move,
In the place of the gossiping psychiatrists who pass
What their patients say around like children playing
Telephone, until the message that said *Help me* has become
The sky has disappeared, leaving nothing in its place,

In the place where bewigged judges disguise themselves as bearded
   psychiatrists,
In the place of rooms that do not lock and of rooms that lock
Only from the outside, in the place of misery beyond telling, in the
   place of weeping
And white fluted flowers that bloom in trays at regular hours, a
   pink or blue
Or golden seed splitting at its heart while the corridors watch your
   every move,

In the place of the talking doctors whose definitions are all syn-
   onyms
And the place of the patients who have nothing to say, since what
   the patients say,
The doctors translate, thinking, because they have been given de-
   grees and because
Their dictionaries may be modified by majority vote at the APA,
   that they understand
The language, in the place where the corridors watch your every
   move,

Someone was saying *Help me help me I am frightened*
Because the sky has disappeared, leaving nothing in its place.

Lady Macbeth on the Psych Ward

Doctor, I'm lost in these mazy halls that lead nowhere,
Sleepwalking through somebody else's nightmare
On Six North, wiping my hands on my hair.

There's blood on my hands, blood in my hair,
Blood between my pale scissoring legs where
It pools in my underpants—the fancy pair

I bought for him to watch me wear and not wear.
There is blood everywhere
And I am lost in it. Doctor, I breathe blood, not air.

Needle and Thread

My swelling breasts are as meant to be touched as silk.
My clitoris is a small spool

Of red thread.
I am fabric, I want to be sewn.

I want your needle stitching my wound.
I want you to lick the end of my thread

And thread me through
And through.

God I want you.
My breasts are like silk

But someone has unwound
My mind and cut off my head.

I am the headless woman
In the hospital bed.

You, I called, when I woke
From the drugged sleep of the still undead, *you.*

Oh you, oh you, I said.

Taking Back the Night (But My Eyes Aren't Blue)

I was prettier then.
My eyes were as blue
As sun on a tin
Roof, and I had you.

My kiss and the dew
Were kith and kin
And kept for you.
I was prettier then.

I had thin skin
Needing to be touched. Everyone knew
You were more than my friend.
My eyes, so blue,

Had nothing to do
With blue nights then.
I danced for you
Like sun on a tin

Roof, kicked off one shoe
And then the other
And then I had you
All night, old brother.

The House at the End of the Road

We are here
in this house
at the end of the road,
behind the sand hill on Route 29,

and because it's warm
today it doesn't matter
that the windows are broken,
cardboard panes checkerboard the January light

and the portable heater
leaks kerosene onto the claptrap floor.
Your face, now fallen from its screen-star (you could have
been) splendor,
shocks me almost into speechlessness

but we manage
the How-Are-You, the We've-Gotten-Older, the
How-Long-Has-It-Been-Let's-See-Six-Years-Isn't-It lines,
and then you say,

reprising an old role, But what did it *mean*
to be a member of our family?—and
your stagy gaze, your flying hair
and clenched fists,

the way you still,
at this pitifully late date, try to dominate
by a confusion of contemptuous condescension
and Only-You-Can-Understand-Me laughter—

drawing me into a secret circle
no one else can penetrate—makes me
want to cry, makes me mask myself
in stock phrases, classic as *Antigone,* and

I hold myself, when
you take me in your arms and hold me, your sister,

apart, I hold myself delicately apart,
        I shut my eyes and pretend

    my skin is not touching
yours, my hand patting your shoulder (a threadbare sweater, no
    Theban shield) is
        somebody else's comforting hand,
          I am not here

        in this house,
the front yard blossoming with mud,
      the Doberman standing guard by the ditch,
         the cold sun planted overhead
            like a gravestone
                in the cemetery of the sky.

The Final Visit with Her Brother

She remembers the drafty rooms,
        the front lawn where mud blooms,

how he lay there, legs like sticks—
        like kindling!—drinking six-

pack beer or "tonic water."
        My eye. Later,

how he insisted on standing and taking her
        in his arms, after making clear

how deeply he felt she'd let him down,
        and said he loved her anyway, but soon

she pulled away, feeling caught
        in the embrace she had fought

so hard to free herself from,
        and he lay back down on the bed and said, "Come

again, you hear?"—softly mocking
        the Southern sense of what is kindly, what is shocking—

and turned the TV on again,
        the black-and-white portable, when

she left, as if to ignore
        the closing of the door.

II

The poem of the mind in the act of finding
What will suffice.

—Wallace Stevens, "Of Modern Poetry"

Text: not a detour, but the flesh at work in a labor of love.

—Hélène Cixous, "Coming to Writing"

An Other Woman

Part One: Waking Alone at Night in Virginia

At night in bed I reach for you, your love.
My hand brushes against an emptiness
Too dark to see; but I feel its sharp edge.
It will cut me if I let it, will wedge
Its way between my knees, kiss me coldly
And leave before I'm through. I'm not sadness' slave,

To let cold darkness live where you have lived.

The room is filled with dreaming moths, and bees
Hang in the spider's web awaiting morning.
I blink my eyes against the unseen room
And tell myself: I'm more than moth, and dream
Of light as you see it, of your warm breath
On my cheek, or your hair lifted now in the car window's breeze.

Part Two: Waking Alone at Night in Virginia, She
Thinks of Him Driving Northeast from Wisconsin
with His Wife and Children

What is the final arrival of which we speak?
Is it that moment when we "squeak, like dolls,
The wished-for words"? Is it that dying time
When, being haunted, the cold gray scattered light
Shuts down, the oboe player puts away
The oboe, and the moon-maddened singer
Walks mute through the garden at last?
                                                            Listen,
Those shadowy roses could tell stories of when
Their petals, like oval heart-tipped plates, held
A dust as delicate as cocaine, their sleeping
Stems were heavy with dreams, and the angel of night
Spread out its wings—thick, patterned tapestries
Seed-pearled with stars—then furled them up again
Into the folded, bright hem of the horizon.
I think of you, your life, your humorous eyes
Bluer than the Charioteer's shining
In all that changing, moving, shifting sky. . . .
Your father and sister are dying, they are planning
To leave you, you are driving cross-country
In time to see the changing of the leaves,
Upstate New York at apple time, the road
Home disappearing under your turning tires.
Do I even know the way to New Hampshire?
I dream the distance every night, I wake
With that highway *whirr* in my head, I see
Your face in profile by the glare of passing
Headlights, I feel your loss and if I could
Would reach out to touch you, would take the wheel
While you sleep in back.
                                        I can't. Your going
From me always is an inevitable season, is
Only another way of telling time.
Roses are red clocks.
                                    Once upon a time,

In Virginia Beach, a soothsayer read
My fortune. It seems that in another life
I had a child, a young daughter accused
Of witchcraft—this was in old New England—
And when they came for her I let them in.
They banged on the door at night, their lanterns
Swaying in blackness, I let them take her,
And it's true I sometimes hear her weeping
In the wind, I remember her adolescent screams,
The grainy grave-dirt raining on her hair,
Which I had washed for her that morning, bending
Her small head under the well-water pump handle.
All these are facts, I'm told, I could not leave
Uncorrected and came back to this world
To amend. At least I mean well, being childless.
Now I wonder: Suppose when you bury
Your father, sister, you should find the bones,
A piece of cloth, belonging to my daughter?
How many bodies does the earth have room for?
Do they touch, secretly under the earth?
Do they hold bony hands, and do they dance
Quietly, or raucously, under their stony crowns?
My mother is afraid of enclosed spaces,
She will not ride in elevators, she
Is unhappy in locked rooms, she will not
Sleep with the window shut. I understand
How she feels, I have been told that sometimes
Our positions in lives are reversed, they say
It's quite possible she was my daughter
Whom I betrayed, we are working these things
Out. Out. Out. Out. Out.
Given time enough, anything is possible,
Even the forgotten assumptions of fathers and daughters.
Even the worst-feared fact, sorrow-bearing
And lethal and powder-white as phencyclidine,
May cast itself in a stunning new form
And what had been an idol be transformed
To living image, as for instance in

The case of the woman who feeds her child
On death, stuffing death down his throat like love.
She's fattening that infant for her table,
She will chew on her baby's bones, and this
Is not a matter of taste, it is a fact
Of ecology. At night, in the dank cellar,
He will sprout eyes like potato eyes, and
His roots will wind through half the house by dawn.
The generations are growing and dying behind
Our backs, beneath our feet.
                                        Your sons will stand
At your father's grave, the coltish wind combing
Their still-blond hair. And as you look from them
To your mother, it will become clear to you
How far you have come and how close you are
Yet; and as you look at her looking down
Into the grave, she abruptly lifts her face.
What you see then must live in my memory
Forever, undelivered and undead.
I see you seeing her fling you away.
You had not thought that she would leave
You so utterly. Her heart is saying:
Husband, and just for this one late moment,
There is no room in that sentence for *son.*
You take her arm, you lead her home.
                                        To New
Hampshire, of course, where I have never been.
I am imagining all this, I could
Be wrong but, *mon amour,* I think that when
You scold your sons, you feel a confusing rush
Of tenderness, as if you would protect
Them from yourself, and as you drive with them
Away from me, your wine-dark wife staring
Silently out the window, remember that
I said those wished-for words, and they were wished for,
Even before you touched me—though also after.

*Part Three: While He Is Still on the Road with His
Wife and Children She Receives the Letter He
Mailed before He Left Wisconsin*

I

Today I wake knowing that I have read
The last letter from you I'll ever read.
It lies on my table; the sun bleaches
That Wisconsin envelope the color of
Whitewashed villas on Greek islands we'll never
See, the color of Jamesian handkerchiefs,
Bridal veils and classic, ironed sheets,
Or less domestically—avoid that hurt—
The color of itself in August, when
Time narrows to the merest thread, seaming
The sky, and noon's a knot of thirty-weight light.

II

This light troubles and stirs me; I am like
The flower on the table, adjacent to
Your last letter. The power of the light
Pries its petals open, touches, kisses
That unsuspecting face. . . . I yank the cord
To shut it out and still the light steals in
Between the slats, it enters through the cracks
At the tops of the windows, it comes in
Boldly by the door. There is no turning
Away from day. There is no turning back.
The power of the light is this: to shine on black.

III

Black worlds. Stars so dense their great gravity
Swallows their light, they feed on their own fullness.
This is a bad joke, a parody of
Creation. Black holes—the poets love it,
They eat that image and spit it back out
In poems. I love it. I eat and eat, I
Will grow fat with despair, thin with despair,
When I look in the mirror I will see

My own shadow, shaking hands with the me
That is not there, the me that said, "Without you,
I am an imitation of myself."

IV

You wrote, "I am holding you in my mind."
I lie in your memory like a woman in bed.
I remember your unclothed body shining
Gold-red in the late afternoon sunlight lining
The walls like wallpaper, the bed like sheets.
I remember your fitting into me
And the street noises on the other side
Of the window. I remember too much,
I will never be able to forget
Your kissing the back of my neck, the way you wrote
Your name between my legs with your fine pen.

V

For days I have sat at my typewriter
Waiting for words that would not come, the blue
Sky going gray each day at four o'clock.
The rain escapes the clouds at four o'clock,
Splashes the green grass, the cows and bullock
In the pasture, Mt. San Angelo's flock
Of sheep, its cats, dogs, field mice, its bright
Humming fences, Queen Anne's lace, wood, clay, rock.
The grass stalk's shadow lies across the ground
And no words live in my brain, but one sound
I remember: your knock on the door of my heart.

VI

Rain light is thin as pewter; it tames my mood,
I may yet become civilized, I am
Your India, your Africa, your South.
The sun after rain spreads and runs, it draws
Cool shadows on the lawn. Your last letter.
I will bring you bourbon and branch water,
Fan your sweating forehead with palmetto leaves,
Or I would, but I have read, as I say,

Your last letter; it arrived yesterday,
And since then I've not been sure of anything
Except the way the light is sliding from my eyes.

VII

Your father and sister are dying: it's too much
To be borne. They are planning to fly away
At midnight, they will take each other's hand
And leave you, they may go to Samarkand
Or Paradise, it's the same thing in the end.
A tip for the tourist: getting there is *all* the fun.
You are driving east to New England, I
Am in Virginia, your last letter came
From Wisc., and the compass I gave you is whirling
Madly in your desk drawer, it can't keep track
Of all these comings and goings, it's too much.

VIII

I cannot write back—your watchful wife would know.
This was the agreement: to quit without
Complaint, when the time came. Your father meets
The contract better than I can, I am grieving
For the light dying at length over the lawn,
The dusk nibbling on day, the picked-clean bones
Of light littering the flower beds, as if
Jerome had killed it, time being one more
Winged morsel, I am grieving for the way
Night murders memory. You do not think
Of me, dream your martyred mother in mink.

IX

And this is as it was to be, Beethoven
Knew that. The last letter, the light woven
Through the turned blinds, the faded sounds, dusky
As a worn Persian rug, of a piano,
Reaching to the single woman's bedroom.
I think of words I cannot write: *Be brave,*
The world is not what it seems, and the last
Letter is never written, the last poem

Requires daring and tact at the entrance
And heaps ending on ending, when compelled
To stop, it changes direction. It begins.

X

It changes direction. It begins. This is
A woman's way of creating, finding rightnesses
In sudden sounds her throat gives, the final note
Love's cry, a single syllable strung on air,
The rising and falling echo of light.
And in that repetition there occurs
The figure of the man she loved then, and
The one she loves now, and drawing the comb
Through her hair, she rises from the bed,
Remembering where she last read love, the words
She tied around her heart with palest thread.

XI

The end of the journey is a crossroads
By moonlight, the rutted clay gold, the sky
Black as a leech. This is the point where you
Go on and I pour myself a drink and think
About the poem of the mind and body that it must
Conceive, it must contain the intent, must say,
"In my mind I am holding you, my arms
Think you, my thighs spell your name, I am writing
The color of your eyes on the inside of my lids."
This is where you say about me, "I met her
In Chicago and later mailed her my last letter."

III

Do you know what I think of pretty often, what I already said to you some time ago—that even if I did not succeed, all the same I thought that what I have worked at will be carried on. Not directly, but one isn't alone in believing in things that are true. And what does it matter personally then!...

The difference between happiness and unhappiness! Both are necessary and useful, as well as death or disappearance...it is so relative—and life is the same.

Even faced with an illness that breaks me up and frightens me, that belief is unshaken.

—Vincent van Gogh in a letter to his brother,
Theo, September 10, 1889

The Model Looks at Her Portrait: A Retrospective

The Lady in Red, on Scarlet, by Betty Watson

Outside the painting, staring at herself
in the painting where she is in this room
she's in while staring guardedly at a painting
like murder, or sex, a painting in which she's in
a room on whose red wall, in the distance,
a man in bathing trunks, waist-deep in blood
or water, stands facing his wife and child
and, as if floating on the water, or
a shoal, a house with castle turrets, lighted
windows, seems both to drift and not to drift,
she sees the long-haired girl she used to be,
in boots and mini-dress, apart and watchful,
as in a redoubt, in a room in a painting in
a room, or as if in a poem turned inside out.

A Frame of Mind

All this color, as if it mattered,
As if forms drawn together
And held apart
By color

Were not—
Viewed in that light that is a true light—
To be seen as one stillness,

The blue tractor alchemized to gold
Along the wheel-rim where it is planted in
The field of rapeseed,

The gold field fading in a gold rush of light,
The sheep, cadmium
In a blue, dissolving distance,
Like white sails of an infinitely slow ship—

A frame of mind
In which the world
Blurs to immobility,
As if speeded down—

And of course,
Everywhere
A blue, blue sky,
Marbled with unmoving clouds.

The Horse at Dusk

He was showing himself off,
switching his tail,
thrusting his lovely head over the fence
and a bit put out when I had no sugar
to give him.
Finally, he bent one foreleg against the other
as in a bow.
Sorrel and rapeseed
sparked like the faintest of flames
in a dusk like smoke
and red poppies had ignited singly
here and there,
as if the fire were spreading.
Blue hills stood not far off,
and in the valley
the small lights of houses
came on.
Trees shook their green manes.

On Looking at a Yellow Wagon

The yellow wagon,
motionless, in the snow-flowering field,
as a windless day,
seems to say, *Whatever enters*
this manifold scene can become part of it, if you let it,
the way a painting of a landscape grows grassblade by grassblade,
those turbulent bushes
scribbled
or thumbprinted
into the lower-right foreground
almost, but not quite,
excessive.

Battle Scene

The blacksmith sun hammered the empty plain
Into a great gold plate: a mere mountain

Wouldn't withstand that onslaught day in and out.
Horse hooves striking the bright rock rang like cut

Glass, and a scorpion darted, like a tongue,
Back and forth, about to sting or having stung.

This was the scene of battle; on either side
Of the plain, in ranked rows, the soldiers tried

To clear their minds and concentrate on death—
Not their own but someone else's valued breath

Brought back like loot. Their shields mirrored the sun,
The sun tipped the head of each javelin

With flame, and in pairs the first line mounted
Chariots drawn by creatures since hunted

To extinction. The reins the driver held
Were painstakingly worked from precious gold,

Silver and lapis lazuli, and where
He drove, his cohort hurled a lighted spear.

By the time the shadows lengthened, cooling
The land like streams of water and pooling

Into darkness, bodies lay everywhere
As if beaten back by the muscular air

Into a vanished age. The scholars dig
Their grave. The dead soldiers' tactical rig

Spins around a painted wall in a frieze
And still spins, after centuries.

The Grecian Grace of a White Egret

Child of bayou country,
My mother could not forget
The darkness upon the face
Of the deep, that the sun set

Before it rose, spirited away
By the waving arms of cypress.
That cypresses had knees.
And floating logs could grow restless,

And crawl up banks.
And she could not forget,
Any more than any lesson of art or history,
The Grecian grace of a white egret,

Its stillness amid the moving mist.
If the death that changes us, changes us
To the forms of our desire,
The wings she wears are not an angel's

And carry her even higher.

Study for an Annunciation

Mary in thought, though her thoughts are free of sin
even in the sinful quattrocento.
An angel's wing as wide and flat as a fin,
as if the announcing angel swam through blue
sky. This wing so richly outlandish, it could be
the glittering keel of a golden boat steered carefully
to shore, where it transformed itself into
something amphibian, whose words she heard
as if they had risen through miles of water, distant
and parsed into syllables like scuba bubbles
and saying merely what she already knew,
that even the perfect life begins below
and not on high, within the flux, the dreamy
flow that had caught her in its undertow.

Virgin and Child

I'll say that there are bits of gold
            stuck in her hair, star-bits, brilliant
                        blue slivers at the edge of the painting
that seem to dance in the light
            from the fire. I'll say there's a fire
                        even though there can't be
and I'll say the painting is as large as a room
            and it can be. She moves in it
                        as if it is a room,
the gold bits gleaming like candles
            that consume nothing, not even themselves.
                        The child crawls out of her arms
and onto the floor
            and his plump wrists
                        and knees
are like loaves of bread,
            his mouth smells of milk,
                        his palms are so tiny
there's no room for even one nail hole.
            She steps out of the frame,
                        her hair sparkling
and the background to everything lapis lazuli and glittering,
            and when she calls to him, clapping
                        and laughing,
he hurtles toward her,
            on all fours of course,
                        and she catches him up
and swings him over her head,
            and her hair with the stars pinned in it
                        and the dancing blue background
slip backward into space
            and it is the child's face
                        risen now, looking down,
into her face,
            mother and son
                        meeting each other's eyes
as we look on.

A Child Is Dying

A child is dying, a child we know.
His dimpled face was as cherubic
as any putto by Della Robbia.

A child is dying, a child we thought would grow
into a man. And his licorice hair and cocoa face
were fair (which means "lovely" and "pleasing").

A toddler, he had a toddler's growing grace.

A child is dying—
our little Homeboy, our sweet Bro'.

He raised his chubby hands to keep the flash
out of his face.
          The photo
shows him squinting and laughing, though
today we are sick
with unforeseen sorrow.

Death outruns art in the human race.

Sunrise

An egret on the river's edge,
    A sky as blue as if it were
The backdrop for a Renaissance
    View of the Ascension (that slow, sure

Stately flight from earthly sorrow
    Into Paradise,
Where angels patrol
    The hallways of God's highrise,

Looking a little like egrets
    Themselves, so long and white
And winged), a morning
    Risen from the night.

Rising Venus

They have it wrong:
I am not young,

was born old enough
to ride the rough

waves of the sea
without drowning, and immodestly.

Semen and seaweed clung
to my hair, hung

on my bare skin
sunstruck and shimmering in

the salt-stunned air.
I had to endure

such heaviness; to push
upward against the rush

of riptide and current.
I said, *I can't*

do this, but I
did it, and I

made it look natural
to float *au naturel,*

easy as the art
of swimming in salt

water, my pelvis fallopian,
eager, the shell scalloped,

the shell's translucent pink
a flat-out Freudian wink.

Did you think that
shell beached itself? That

a breeze as soft
as a hand luffed

my long hair and
breathed me onto land?

And when I reached
shore, I yanked leeches

from my legs, dredged
sand from armpits, cadged

food from scavenging birds.
I learned the words

I would need here.
Learned want, learned fear

and how to live
with both. (How? Forgive

yourself for being mortal.)
Myth is the portal

through which we pass,
becoming human at last,

rising out of dream
and desire to realms

of reality, where love,
a woman, by Jove,

survives, strong and free,
engendering her own destiny.

Romantic Art

The light, ripped out of the sky
And flung into a field, field of an eye, field of vision—

The muddy path winds along the gorge
Trailing rhododendron and white
Wood violets, forget-me-nots
Forgotten at the bitter edge,

While far below, the river, foaming, rabid,
Hurls itself against rocks—

The light, lying in the grass and ferns,
Cast off, orphaned—

A young woman beats back branches with a stick,
Her hair cropped short as a boy's,
Her knuckles red with cold

(It's late in the day, late in the history of the world)

She hears a noise, turns—

She is in a painting like opera,
All aria and deceptive show,
The sounds too bright,
Herself in shadow

The Color Red

A breeze fluttered her hem around her ankles.
Her parasol made her face swim in a pool of shade.
The little dog, so happy to be alive and there, asked to be held.
This was—I don't know—1881.

A century ago.

The color red permeated everything:
    Her smooth, flushed cheeks.
    The ribbon on her bonnet.
    The nearly translucent inside of the dog's attentive ears.
    The sky (though not yet sunset).

The color red had even seeped into the future, where it would
    become politics.
    And blood.

But this was—what—1881.
And she was only a girl, barely eighteen,
    And the breeze
    And the parasol
    And the small bundle of dog
Were more than she could handle
    Without laughing.

So she laughed.

And I can hear her laughter.

Oriental Nude

She lay in light, as if a light-
weight coverlet had billowed down
over her to keep off the chill,
since she would not fool with nightgown
or kimono, and yet she seemed
so inscrutable she might have been
the author of a book called *Zen and*
The Art of Being Comfortable in Your Own Skin.

On Looking at a Painting by van Gogh

The blue sky is a priceless porcelain pitcher
from which light pours itself,
cooling the canvas, serene benediction
of brightness, the long green throat
of the cypress stretching thirstily toward azure.

Now look again, at the bigger picture,
the one in which you observe yourself
alone in a place in the sun
that is no place, in a field of blowing, sun-blanched wheat.
The blue sky appalls, it is too pure

for words. A thousand, or more or fewer,
will not describe by half
the way you felt when you stood there, knowing someone
or something had framed you and you would be taking the heat
for that one careless day for much longer than you could ever
    endure.

The Cypress (Fiesole)

1

I am beauty.
I am silence's silhouette, dark
green against a darkening sky,
stark

as a reminder—say, of something
you wished to forget, some humiliating desire,
some subtle, unending burning.
My heart is fire-

wood, I am a green flame
lighting the hillside at day's close.
Beauty's name
is mine, my fame hers.

2

And I am the austere candle,
the moon my wick.
Night puts me out: I'm a mere stick,
beauty's greatest scandal.

Miracle at Giverny

A light unseen shines everywhere,
On the banks, the bridge, and *la petite mer*,
Turning white water lilies to wine,
Water to air.

Rothko

The paintings were of what wasn't there,
as if of the shadow of air.

It smothered you like a pillow, or plastic,
that air you painted, dark and drastic

as all absence, all loss.
And we who live on, because

you painted it cannot avert our eyes.
We see, everywhere, peripheries,

sharpened edges shading into something
as sad as suicide, or painting nothing.

Wishing I Could Bring You Back and See Things More Clearly This Time Around

(Jonathan Silver, sculptor, d. 1992)

I wish that I could bring you back, and you
would be as young as you were then, excited
about the world and art, and loving to
go on about both with me ready to write it
all down. I was enthralled by every word
you said, on any subject—though not always
agreeing and then you said I hadn't *heard*
you but I had, and I still do, some days,
when a painting speaks to me, or when the world
itself seems like a painting, or a sculpture
you might have made (a thing that can seem hurled
at the viewer, light and shade chiseled to pure
pain, as if pain were what we need to see
and what I failed to see, listening so intently).

American Movies

How you had climbed into your pickup truck
like a cowboy, and sung some old song,
        slow as rewinding a tape,
about missed possibility—

Never thinking—
        not once—
never thinking of what might be,
but there were other possibilities
and you had lit out for them
as if for the frontier—

2

In the other movie, the one I saw,
there was a white frame house,
a fan of zinnias in a dark green cough-medicine bottle
on the bookshelf, kittens
in a basket.

And there were flashbacks, which made us younger,
the house still so new to us
it was a language we were learning.

Later,
before dawn,
a trip to the barn
for milk for the baby—

In the kitchen, his embroidered bibs—

(But I don't forget your one silk shirt,
        wrapped in brown paper in the bottom drawer.

Or, after supper, after the washing-up,
your stripped back, smooth and cool as a silver dollar,
shoulder blades like gears,
        grinding, slipping—

Your slipping into bed beside me—

Your waist tapering, legs
        locked into mine—

Quietly, because of the baby—

The steady tick of wind in the grass in the country on a summer
    night,
        that starry-eyed clock—

How, before we slept, we promised each other we would dream the
    same dream;
        in the morning, unspool the same sweet reel—)

Perspective

Three does stood at the edge of the road.
Can Beauty draw breath? They were like lovers' sighs
(If lovers' sighs were visible and stock-still
In air as transparent as lovers' lies).

November blue pressed down
On their frightened, alerted heads;
The earth pushed up to meet their hooves.
Three watchful does were the point where perspective leads,

The vanishing point,
And then they vanished, like breath—
Blown, like alibis—
And that is all of Beauty's Truth.

IV

To a Young Woman

On the occasion of her graduation from Vanderbilt University

The mothers and the fathers mill among magnolias.
Tenderly, the fathers cradle Styrofoam cups
Of coffee in their hands.
                                    The mothers open slick,
Sun-bright umbrellas as the rain begins to fall.
The rain's a soft and slow shower, and whole, single
Drops of it pause, like divers on their diving boards,
Upon the darkening green leaves, the dogwood blooms,
The boles of high-reaching hackberries.
                                    Now, shy ghosts
Of Southern writers are nearly seen before vanishing:
Robert Penn Warren, memorizing three *thousand*
Lines of poetry in his first semester here;
And highbrowed Allen Tate, the great proselytizer
Of all his close friends' poetry; and Cleanth Brooks,
The critic of a generation, Randall Jarrell,
Himself haunted by crueler ghosts.

                              Almost summer
This far south. In Wisconsin, it was still winter.

The casual rain could be a kind of country song,
A simple tune, something picked out on a dulcimer
Or polished, upright piano, so deliberate
And careful, and the air—the air!—seems vaguely green,
As though dye ran from laundered leaves spread like T-shirts
Against the sky.
                        Your proud father ("Vanderbilt Dad,"
Proclaims a green T-shirt he knew better than to wear
Today) will keep a lookout for your appearance
On stage while also, we admit, trying to read—
Over the squared shoulder of yet another father,
One with a newspaper in his lap—the outcome of
The final game of chess played between Kasparov
And the computer known as Deep Blue.
                                    Magnolia

Blossoms infuse the rain with scent, powerfully,
Delicately—a naturally occurring tea.
I miss the South, its exotic perfumes and palette,
The way one moves through the weather here, wearing it
Next to the freed body like chiffon. (In Wisconsin,
The weather is what moves through you, replacing bones
With icicles.) I miss this world of poetry,
And celebrate your being part of its history
Though you are an Econ. major, shrewder than the rest of us
(But once I wrote a poem about one Mr. John,
Professor of the subject and a lonesome man),
And yesterday evening, when your beaming dad
Draped around your neck the pearls that were our present
To you—small, real pearls—and snapped shut the small gold clasp,
Settling the strand around his princess's clavicle,
I wished that I could tell you that you enter your life
Of work surrounded by love, a rich necklace of love,
Because you do, you know, as do all the others, yes,
You *all.* Say that you are tall and beautiful and
Lesbian, writing poems in New York City. Say
That you are small, intense, a girl in a green dress
Working in a bank to buy time to write poetry.
Or you are the sweetly goofy girl who sleeps through
The first half of every class, or the adventurous
Girl who has found her future in her Jewish past
And plans to emigrate to Israel . . . students
Of mine, young women with the gifts and energy
To save a world, if they could believe it—believe
That love is their companion always, that they are loved,
And they are, and you are, but how hard it can be
To know this, for to know it, you must learn it for
Yourself. And not just once but many times, until
Even if you wanted to forget it—but who
Would ever choose to forget it?—you would not be
Able to, you know it so well that knowing it
Is who you are, it is the subject that is you

Remembering, no longer what is remembered.
Thereby do we create the world in which we live,
A world of love and loving.
                              It can and will be that
For you—in any circumstance—if you will let
Yourself surrender to your own ability
To love. I tell you, there is an economy in this,
The way love returns—and if it does not, if—crazy
Thought, but it occurs—you are quite sure that you are unworthy
Of loving—not only of being loved but of loving—
A thought that can burn the brain beyond recovery—
Read this to rediscover the one truth eternal
As time, which is that kindness is irresistible.
Be kind, and you will find even you love yourself—
That is how irresistible kindness is.
                              It
Has power to compel all things to fly toward
The center, bringing difference into unity—

Power of form, the power to shape and hold a world
As intricate and various as ours, or art
Or reasoning, the power of poetry.

At last we hear your name over the loudspeaker
And when, in cap and gown, you walk across the boards
And change the cap's tassel to the other side (charming!),
We are lifted out of our seats to shout congratulations.
Your father's face is filled with love and admiration.

I so wish that you could see him, see how excited
He is for you—

                    You do, later, amid the mob
Beneath the tent, where parents cheer their suddenly
Grown children—when did they become so formidable
And adult? how could it all happen so fast?—with champagne
And strawberries, but do you know how lovely you are

In your donnish get-up, the pearls blossoming at your throat. . . .

The rain has stopped, the cameras click ceaselessly,
A rain-splotched, folded newspaper lies forgotten on
A folding chair, with scores that nobody thinks to turn
To.
      Commencement programs flutter and scatter like pigeons.
People disperse. . . . Swiftly now, the lawn empties,
Families packing into cars, you are leaving,
We are leaving, sunlight stumbling across the lawn,
The campus left to its dreams of solitude and staying
Up late to study, even economics, the
Flowering dogwood wearing white petals like pearls,
Pearls strewn on grass, the pearls of wisdom, if the will
Matures and gives itself to the idea of
Itself.